ADVENTURES IN KINDNESS

52 Awesome Kid Adventures for Building a Better World

Written by
Sophia Fox and Carrie Fox

Illustrated by
Nichole Wong Forti

Printed in the United States of America
First Edition

Book Design and Production: Anne C. Kerns, Eleni Stamoulis
Illustration: Nichole Wong Forti

Adventures in Kindness is a publication of Mission Partners Press, a division of Mission Partners, Benefit LLC. **adventuresinkindness.com**

ISBN: 978-1-7346186-0-0

"Do your little bit of
good where you are;
it's those little bits of good
put together that
overwhelm the world."

Desmond Tutu

To Kate and Brian,
and all the adventures
that lie ahead.

CONTENTS

Hi Friend!

When we set out to write this book, we didn't know exactly where our writing adventure would take us. But after having one too many conversations trying to make sense of mean acts, we decided it was time to build a list of what we—kids and adults—could do to put more good in the world—in every way imaginable. We developed *Adventures in Kindness* as a practical resource for kids and their families who care about doing good in the world, and who might enjoy connecting with other kind kids too.

While writing *Adventures in Kindness*, we tested and completed many of the adventures included in the book, and here's what stuck with us most: With every adventure we took on, we felt our hearts fill up with happiness. We felt more aware of the world around us. We felt surprised and wanting to learn even more about the people we met, the places we went, and the cultures we experienced along the way. Our hope is that the adventures in this book leave you feeling the same way.

You are now part of a special group of kids, doing a world of good. We hope you'll share details of your adventures with us. As soon as you've finished your first adventure, you can hop online (with the help of a parent or caring adult) to **adventuresinkindness.com** to officially join the ranks of the Adventures in Kindness Kids Club. After five completed adventures, you can earn a free backpack badge. And, if you share one of your own adventures in kindness, not included in this book, you'll be entered to win an Adventures in Kindness t-shirt from our kindness store, and you may be featured in a future edition of *Adventures in Kindness*.

KIND IS COOL. LET'S LIVE IT PROUDLY.

To many good adventures ahead,

Sophia Fox

Sophia Fox
4th grade, co-author

Carrie Fox

Carrie Fox
mom, co-author

This is more than a book.
It's a community of kind kids.

If you're like us, you're a curious kid with a desire to do good in the world around you. Well, good news. This is just the book for you.

With 50+ ideas on how to improve the world around you—big ideas, little ideas and everything-in-between ideas—you've got a lot of ways to keep you kind and busy. You can either take each week's adventure in order, or just flip through the book and see what looks good based on your mood.

As you flip though the pages, you'll see that every adventure in this book is organized into one of nine cool categories:

⭐ ANIMALS	⭐ HEALTH	⭐ COMMUNITY
⭐ KIDS	⭐ WORLD	⭐ SCHOOL
⭐ FAMILY	⭐ MIND	⭐ TROOPS

Just look for the section of the book you're most interested in, and dig right in.

There is just one thing we ask: remember to take notes about each one of your world-changing adventures so you have a record of what you did and how it made you feel. This book doesn't end at the back cover. In fact, that's just the beginning.

If you want to connect with a whole community of kind kids, we hope you'll join us over at **adventuresinkindness.com**, where you'll find useful tools and resources to help complete your adventures, and a place to submit your own adventure, which might just end up in a future edition of this book.

KEEP ON READING
TO LEARN MORE!

ADVENTURES

FOR
ANIMALS

"Whatever you are, be a good one."

Abraham Lincoln

Did you know that you can help animals no matter how old you are? There are millions of dogs, cats, bunnies, and other animals in shelters right now, waiting for their forever homes, and there are so many ways for you to help them.

Adventure 1

Volunteer at Your Local Animal Shelter

Around 70,000 puppies and kittens are born in the U.S. every day,[1] and there are nowhere near enough good homes for all of them. Many of them will spend most, if not all, of their lives in shelters just waiting for an opportunity to have a forever home.

Whether you're able to have a pet at home or not, you can still do something special and kind for the animals in your local shelter.

If you find a shelter that will let you volunteer, you can walk dogs, clean up after the animals, refill water bowls, and give out toys and treats. Even just being there to pet cats and scratch dogs behind the ears will help them feel less lonely.

TiP! While visiting, ask if your local shelter has any particular supplies they're in need of, such as old towels, t-shirts, animal food or toys, that you can help collect through a neighborhood or school drive.

Keep in mind that you may need a bit of help from a family member or friend with this one, since some shelters require that all kids be accompanied by an adult.

→ **What You May Need to Complete this Adventure:**

Adult supervision

Assorted craft supplies, old towels or t-shirts, or pet toys

Approximate time: one to three hours

Cost: none – $

REPORT FROM THE FIELD

I completed this adventure on this date:

My adventure took place at:

I had help from the following people:

This adventure made me feel:

What I loved most about this adventure:

One thing I learned from this adventure:

One thing that surprised me about this adventure:

One thing I don't want to forget about this adventure:

Play an Active Role in Preserving Our Oceans

Whether you live near an ocean or smack dab in the middle of America you can play an active part in protecting our oceans and all the sea creatures that call them home. First, make a commitment to give up single-use plastic items such as plastic snack bags, plastic forks, plastic water bottles, and most importantly, plastic straws. America alone uses over 500 million plastic straws every day,[2] and most of those end up in our oceans, polluting the water and killing marine life. If we don't work together to end the use of plastic straws, by 2050 there will be more plastic in the ocean than there are fish.[3]

Take this adventure in kindness one step further by keeping a sturdy, reusable beach pail or bucket and gardening or work gloves with your beach or vacation bag. Anytime you are near a beach, pond, or lake, take a few minutes away from building sandcastles or splashing in the water to remove any trash you find that could harm local sea creatures. Make it a point to simply leave every beach area you visit **cleaner than the way you found it**. You could even organize a community-wide clean-up day and start by asking three friends to help! Any way you go about it, you're doing good for the sea and all the creatures who call it home.

➜ What You May Need to Complete this Adventure:

Dinner time conversation with family; agree together to give up single-use plastic!

Sturdy, reusable beach pail or bucket and garden or work gloves (both of which can be found at the dollar store)

Approximate time: ten minutes to two hours; though this adventure can become part of your everyday actions

Cost: $

REPORT FROM THE FIELD

I completed this adventure on this date:

My adventure took place at:

I had help from the following people:

This adventure made me feel:

What I loved most about this adventure:

One thing I learned from this adventure:

One thing that surprised me about this adventure:

One thing I don't want to forget about this adventure:

Set Up a Donation Drive

Ask your teacher, school principal or PTA president if you can lead a donation drive at your school for a local nonprofit animal shelter or humane society. You and your family members can write a letter or email telling your school officials how you plan on doing it and why it is important to collect items that animals in shelters need, such as food, toys, leashes, beds, and blankets. In your letter or email, make sure to include:

⭐ Why you think your school or PTA should organize a donation drive for the local animal shelter.

⭐ Why you are passionate about animals, and what you think can happen if your school gets involved.

⭐ What you are asking for: space inside the building to put the donation box? Support from student council to get the word out?

⭐ How you think the students at school can help with the donation drive.

⭐ Who is involved and what roles they would like to play?

⭐ When you hope to hold the donation drive, and for how long.

Once the donation drive details are set, get a group of your friends and classmates together to make colorful posters so you can spread the word about the donation drive!

➡ **What You May Need to Complete this Adventure:**

Support from school or community center

Promotional flyers and posters

Approximate time: one day to one month

Cost: $–$$

REPORT FROM THE FIELD

I completed this adventure on this date:

My adventure took place at:

I had help from the following people:

This adventure made me feel:

What I loved most about this adventure:

One thing I learned from this adventure:

One thing that surprised me about this adventure:

One thing I don't want to forget about this adventure:

Offer to Walk the Dog or Sit with the Cat of an Older or Sick Neighbor

If you know that one of your neighbors is ill, or maybe they're getting older and having a hard time giving their animal the walking and play time it needs, consider offering some regular animal-sitting or walking help. Even one walk per week could make a big difference and it helps your neighbor as well as your neighbor's pet.

Not sure how to find someone who could use this service? Make a flyer letting your neighbors and friends know of your service, and drop it in your neighbors' mailboxes or post it on your community's bulletin board. Also, let your friends and teachers know of your interest to help and see if they can introduce you to someone in the neighborhood who might really appreciate your service.

➡ What You May Need to Complete this Adventure:

Approval from your parent or guardian and approval from your neighbor

Approximate time: 15–20 minutes per walk

Cost: none

A NOTE FROM SOPHiA

When you set out on this adventure, just remember to be gentle with the animal, and always ask a dog's owner before you go to pet it, as some dogs aren't comfortable with strangers.

REPORT FROM THE FIELD

I completed this adventure on this date:

My adventure took place at:

I had help from the following people:

This adventure made me feel:

What I loved most about this adventure:

One thing I learned from this adventure:

One thing that surprised me about this adventure:

One thing I don't want to forget about this adventure:

Adventure 5

Host a Community Dog Wash

Who doesn't love a squeaky clean pup? Gather your friends or family members to host a one-day community dog wash, where four-legged friends can get a bath in exchange for a donation such as a toy or towel for a local shelter or humane society.

For this adventure, you'll need access to: a hose, several bottles of dog shampoo, and old towels. You can set up stations for dog owners to wash their own dogs or you can offer to wash the dogs. Just make sure the dog's owner is present to keep the animal on a leash and under control.

➡️ **What You May Need to Complete this Adventure:**

Adult supervision

Water source and hose, large bins to use as baths, and dog shampoo

Bins to collect donations

Promotional flyers and posters

Approximate time: at least two weeks to plan, prepare and host dog wash

Cost: $$ – $$$

REPORT FROM THE FIELD

I completed this adventure on this date:

My adventure took place at:

I had help from the following people:

This adventure made me feel:

What I loved most about this adventure:

One thing I learned from this adventure:

One thing that surprised me about this adventure:

One thing I don't want to forget about this adventure:

— ADVENTURES —
FOR KIDS

"Be kind whenever possible. It is always possible."

Dalai Lama

In every city, community, and school, there are kids going through challenging times. Maybe someone is fighting a difficult sickness, feeling lonely, or being bullied. Maybe someone doesn't have access to a safe and stable home or healthy food. Maybe someone is simply feeling down and could use some kindness from you today.

Make a Sick Kid's Day

For children suffering from serious illnesses and long hospital stays, any contact with the outside world can bring a smile to their face. Young patients undergoing chemotherapy or radiation are often unable to be around their friends, classmates, or other children because their immune systems are weak. They miss out on everyday kid activities like going to the movies, attending sporting events, celebrating birthday parties, and trick-or-treating in their neighborhood.

Send some cheer to a kid battling a tough sickness by drawing a picture, writing a letter, or building a birthday box through one of these nonprofit organizations:

Cards for Hospitalized Kids
cardsforhospitalizedkids.com
Cards for Hospitalized Kids (CFHK) is an internationally recognized charitable organization that spreads hope, joy, and magic to hospitalized kids across the U.S. through uplifting, handmade cards. Anyone can get involved, from anywhere, by making handmade cards and sending them to the CFHK office for distribution in hospitals and Ronald McDonald Houses across the nation. Since this organization's founding, they've helped deliver cards to over 100,000 kids in hospitals in all 50 states. Help them keep that number growing!

Hope for Henry Foundation
hopeforhenry.org
Deliver a happiness kit or a birthday party in a box to a sick child. The Hope for Henry Foundation was founded by Henry Strongin Goldberg's parents after he died at age 7 following complications from a bone marrow transplant. But the spirit of Henry is alive and well in this Foundation. To date, Hope for Henry has hosted special events for more than 45,000 patients and their siblings including Halloween parties, superhero celebrations, birthday parties, book parties, movie days, spa parties, and visits from professional athletes.

A NOTE FROM SOPHiA

No one likes to feel sick, so use this adventure to bring a good distraction and a happy moment to a kid who needs it.

Not sure what to say in the card?
Here are a few suggestions:

1. You are so strong and brave!

2. You've got this.

3. Keep on fighting.

4. You're my favorite superhero.

Consider adding a drawing to the card or include some of your favorite jokes to help bring a smile to their face.

REPORT FROM THE FIELD

I completed this adventure on this date:

My adventure took place at:

I had help from the following people:

This adventure made me feel:

What I loved most about this adventure:

One thing I learned from this adventure:

One thing that surprised me about this adventure:

One thing I don't want to forget about this adventure:

Adventure 7
Make Healthy Snacks to Share with Your Friends

Who doesn't love a yummy after-school snack? Instead of going for a bag of chips or cookies, experiment with making some healthy snack options and share them with your friends.

What makes a snack healthy? Generally, if you focus on foods that are low in added fat and sugar and high in fiber and water, you'll be making a healthy choice, such as an apple over a bag of chips, some whole-grain crackers with low fat cheese over nachos, or Greek yogurt with granola or fruit over ice cream.

A few more healthy foods to try: How about homemade, no-bake granola bars; or trail mix with nuts, raisins, and seeds. Even homemade ice pops made from 100% juice or a smoothie made from bananas, berries, and yogurt are smart choices for your growing body.

Find at least two recipes that look good, add the necessary items to your family's grocery list and with adult help, make them to replace two of your less healthy snack options.

TIP! Need some yummy inspiration? Check out some of our favorite kid-friendly recipes in *Cooking Class*, a kid's cookbook by Deanna F. Cook. Check it out online at deannafcook.com/cooking-class.

➡ What You May Need to Complete this Adventure:

Adult supervision

Access to a kitchen and kitchen supplies

Approximate time: 30 minutes to one hour per recipe

Cost: $ – $$

A NOTE FROM SOPHIA

Some of my favorite healthy snacks are fresh fruit like apples, strawberries, or whatever is in season. I'll mix them all together and make my own fruit salad for an easy after school snack. I love smoothies, too. My favorite is strawberry-blueberry-banana, with yogurt. Sometimes we even throw in a little kale or spinach, which is ok by me because you can't taste it at all!

Sophia's Favorite
Strawberry-Blueberry-Banana Smoothie

(Makes enough for 2 kid-sized smoothies)

¼ cup of non-fat plain or vanilla yogurt (we use Greek yogurt)
¼ cup of fresh blueberries (or frozen if they're not in season)
5 fresh or frozen strawberries
1 banana
¼ cup orange juice
3 – 4 ice cubes

1. Add yogurt to the blender. Do this first because it blends the fruit easier.
2. Add banana, strawberries and blueberries.
3. Add orange juice and ice cubes.
4. Blend for 60 seconds or until blended to desired consistency.
5. Enjoy!

REPORT FROM THE FIELD

I completed this adventure on this date:

My adventure took place at:

I had help from the following people:

This adventure made me feel:

What I loved most about this adventure:

One thing I learned from this adventure:

One thing that surprised me about this adventure:

One thing I don't want to forget about this adventure:

Adventure 8

Bring Comfort to Kids in Foster Care

On any given day, there are more than 430,000 young people in the foster care system in the United States.[4] Of the thousands of young people who enter the foster care system each year, most arrive carrying little more than the clothes on their backs. For the kids who collect personal belongings while in foster care, such as clothes, backpacks, or other personal items, most will be given nothing more than a trash bag to carry their items from one home to the next. Many young people in foster care will be moved from home to home multiple times, carrying their life's treasures in that trash bag. But you can help bring comfort and kindness to kids through some of their most difficult days.

Comfort Cases is a national nonprofit that believes every child deserves to feel a sense of dignity and every child deserves to pack their belongings in a special bag that they can call their own. It is the mission of Comfort Cases to provide a proper bag, filled with comfort and essential items, to these brave young people in foster care on their journey to find their forever home. Learn more and organize your own donation drive at comfortcases.org.

TIP! For more ideas on how to help kids in foster care, visit togetherwerise.org to search for local service activities or to bring a service activity for your community.

➡️ **What You May Need to Complete this Adventure:**

Adult supervision

- -

A variety of supplies (visit websites above to learn more)

- -

Approximate time: one day to one week

- -

Cost: $$–$$$

REPORT FROM THE FIELD

I completed this adventure on this date:

My adventure took place at:

I had help from the following people:

This adventure made me feel:

What I loved most about this adventure:

One thing I learned from this adventure:

One thing that surprised me about this adventure:

One thing I don't want to forget about this adventure:

Collect Pennies for Kids with Cancer

When the actor and entertainer Danny Thomas was working to open St. Jude Children's Research hospital in Memphis, Tenn., in the 1950s, he would often say that he'd rather collect a dollar from one million people than $1 million from one person. It's what many people now call "the power of the collective"—a lot of people working together for a cause can make a gigantic impact.

While fighting diseases like cancer takes a lot of people and a lot of money, every dollar and every penny makes a difference. In fact, St. Jude Children's Research Hospital's popular penny fundraisers have raised millions of pennies from kids just like you who wanted to lend a hand in helping to fund cures for cancer.

For this act of kindness, simply find a jar at home and turn it into a collection jar for your spare change. Set a goal to raise $20 before your next birthday, for instance, and then once you've hit the goal, ask your parents or guardian if they can help you donate it to St. Jude Children's Research Hospital or the children's charity of your choice.

TiP! Learn more about how to organize a fundraiser for St. Jude at stjude.org/get-involved/school-fundraising-ideas.

➔ **What You May Need to Complete this Adventure:**

Small jar to collect pennies

Pennies and spare change

Approximate time: one week to one year

Cost: none

REPORT FROM THE FIELD

I completed this adventure on this date:

My adventure took place at:

I had help from the following people:

This adventure made me feel:

What I loved most about this adventure:

One thing I learned from this adventure:

One thing that surprised me about this adventure:

One thing I don't want to forget about this adventure:

Adventure 10
Send Someone a Happiness Kit

If you've noticed that a new kid in school is having trouble making friends or if a neighbor or family member has been feeling blue, send them a happiness kit.

Start with an old shoebox, mug, or a spare basket. (Maybe you can rescue a cardboard box before it makes it to your recycling bin!) Next, fill it with a few things that you think might bring this person joy. Consider including a joke book, a mug with a smiley face on it, some fresh fruit, a kindness rock (see Adventure #46) or other items you think they'll enjoy. Finish it off with a handwritten note of kindness to the person who is feeling blue.

When it's all ready, leave it in a place where you know your friend will find it.

→ What You May Need to Complete this Adventure:

Craft supplies to decorate the box

Gently-used books to pass along

A shoe box or other small box

Approximate time: one day to one week

Cost: $–$$

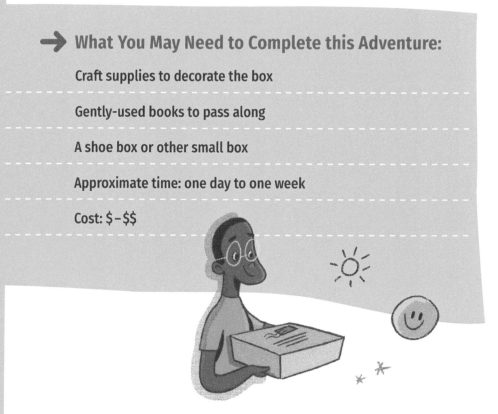

REPORT FROM THE FIELD

I completed this adventure on this date:

My adventure took place at:

I had help from the following people:

This adventure made me feel:

What I loved most about this adventure:

One thing I learned from this adventure:

One thing that surprised me about this adventure:

One thing I don't want to forget about this adventure:

FOR FAMILY

"Never be so busy
as not to
think of others."

Mother Theresa

In our home, we have the Fox Family Rules framed right next to our kitchen table. We developed the rules as a family, and you might not be surprised that the very first rule is to "Be Kind." Our last rule is "Family Comes First," and we work very hard to protect that rule—even on days that feel so busy with school, activities, and friends. This next set of adventures is designed to help you put family first, too.

Start a Family Giving Jar

One thing we love about kindness is that it can often be done as a family. In the lead up to one or more of your family's most celebrated holidays, consider how kindness could become a family tradition. First, find an empty jar—it can be a pickle jar, a peanut butter jar, a Mason jar, or any other jar you have lying around. That's your Giving Jar.

For the entire month leading up to your family's holiday, make it a tradition to place a few pennies or a few dollars—anything considered spare change—in the jar at the end of each day. Then, the week before your big holiday, select someone who's going through a tough time financially and work as a family to give the jar to them in person or anonymously—or donate the collected funds to a nonprofit of your family's choosing.

➡ What You May Need to Complete this Adventure:

An empty, clean jar

Spare change

Approximate time: 30 days to one year

Cost: $–$$$

A NOTE FROM SOPHIA ☆

This is one of my favorite adventures in kindness because you work together as a family and you get to decide together where your giving jar money is needed most. My sister and I started by decorating the jar and then we made it the centerpiece of our kitchen table, so it was easy to think about it (and add to it) almost every day.

REPORT FROM THE FIELD

I completed this adventure on this date:

My adventure took place at:

I had help from the following people:

This adventure made me feel:

What I loved most about this adventure:

One thing I learned from this adventure:

One thing that surprised me about this adventure:

One thing I don't want to forget about this adventure:

Adventure 12

Visit at Least Five Museums, Historic Sites, or Monuments this Year

An important part of being kind is taking time to learn about the people, cultures, and history of the world all around you. Museums, national parks, historic sites, and monuments are all a great source of that learning. Plus, they're the perfect places for special memory-making days with your family.

First, explore the list of museums, national parks, historic sites and monuments near you, and choose at least five that you've never visited before.

TiP! Check out the National Park Service (nps.gov) for a complete list of parks, historic sites, and monuments in your state, including lots of good ideas to help plan your trip.

Then, work with your family to plan day trips or weekend excursions to each one over the course of the year ahead. At each stop along your adventure, take note of the art and artifacts you see, and read about the history of new places you visit. Share with your family what surprised you most about each exhibit or space you explored. Use every new museum or park experience to ask questions and learn alongside your family.

We bet that even before your five-stop adventure is up, you'll be ready to start planning your next round!

YAY

Golden Gate Bridge

Lincoln memorial

Adult supervision

Public transportation

Camera, sketch pad, or journal

Approximate time: three to five hours per museum visit

Cost: none – $$

A NOTE FROM SOPHiA

Whenever I'm headed to a museum with my family, I make sure to pack a full bottle of water and a camera or a sketchbook to help remember some of my favorite things. I also like to go through the museum slowly so I can see lots of what it has to show.

It seems like there's never enough time to do it all, so plan ahead and research the exhibits or special programs that might be available to help make the most of your visit.

Museums are a good place to learn and understand the good and the bad about our world so be ready to ask questions, even if your parents don't have the answers right away. I remember visiting the National Museum of African American History and Culture in Washington, DC, and seeing an exhibit that surprised me about our country's past. I saw many things that made me confused, too. There was a lot that was hard to understand, but it gave our family a lot to talk about afterwards.

REPORT FROM THE FIELD

I completed this adventure on this date:

My adventure took place at:

I had help from the following people:

This adventure made me feel:

What I loved most about this adventure:

One thing I learned from this adventure:

One thing that surprised me about this adventure:

One thing I don't want to forget about this adventure:

Adventure 13

Picture Your Ideal World and Identify What Stands in the Way of Achieving It

Being the change you wish to see in the world starts by envisioning what your kindest version of the world would look like. Work alone, with friends, or with family members to build a list of some of the problems that exist in the world today.

First, draw a line down the center of a white sheet of paper. On the top of one column write **problem**. And on the top of the other column, write **ideal world**.

Then, after you list the problems, jot down what you believe would look different about that problem in your ideal world. For instance, if homelessness is one of the problems you list, you could write that in your ideal world, everyone has a safe home, a warm bed, and a loving family.

When you're done, reflect on your ideal world statements. How do people live? Does everyone have enough to eat? How is the planet being taken care of? Discuss with your family what some of the barriers are to achieving that ideal world and how your family can work together towards your vision for the ideal world.

A NOTE FROM SOPHiA

I loved this adventure because it gave me a chance to see the world like I envision it. I did this adventure with my Girl Scout Troop. I worked with my friends to envision a world with no air pollution, where everyone has a home, and where everyone has access to good education.

Not only did we talk about our ideal worlds, but it gave me more confidence to start making my vision come true.

➡️ What You May Need to Complete this Adventure:

Family or friend to join you in the conversation

Paper and a pen

Approximate time: 20 minutes to two hours

Cost: none

Start brainstorming some ideas below!

PROBLEM   IDEAL WORLD

REPORT FROM THE FIELD

I completed this adventure on this date:

My adventure took place at:

I had help from the following people:

This adventure made me feel:

What I loved most about this adventure:

One thing I learned from this adventure:

One thing that surprised me about this adventure:

One thing I don't want to forget about this adventure:

Create a 100 Days of Gratitude List

One way we love to be kind is by practicing gratitude. That can mean saying thank you at least once each day to someone who has helped you. It can also mean pausing before each night's meal to share one or two things from the day that you're thankful for. We love to do this activity as a family, and you may find that it becomes a tradition for your family too.

Here's a good way to start: keep a journal or notebook right by your bed. At the end of each day, as you're winding down for bed, open the notebook and jot down something (or someone) that you are grateful for. Sometimes, just the act of noticing all that you are thankful for can make us more kind.

➡ What You May Need to Complete this Adventure:

Family or friend to join you in the conversation

Notebook to write down your gratitude statements

Approximate time: two to five minutes per day

Cost: none

1 2 3... ☆

REPORT FROM THE FIELD

I completed this adventure on this date:

My adventure took place at:

I had help from the following people:

This adventure made me feel:

What I loved most about this adventure:

One thing I learned from this adventure:

One thing that surprised me about this adventure:

One thing I don't want to forget about this adventure:

Explore a World Calendar of Holidays with Your Friends or Family

You probably know most of the holidays that your family celebrates, but have you ever thought about the hundreds of other religious and cultural holidays that people celebrate around the world? Wouldn't it be fun to learn more about them?

For this adventure, work with an adult to print out a world calendar of holidays. Then, explore the list and pick one holiday per month that you'd like to know more about.

As each holiday approaches, sit down with your family to learn more about the history and traditions of that holiday. Head to the library and find a book that will teach you more about the holiday or try finding someone in your school or neighborhood who celebrates the holiday and ask them more about it.

A simple calendar of holidays can lead to great conversations about different types of cultures and their celebrations.

➡️ **What You May Need to Complete this Adventure:**

Family or friend to join you in the conversation

Access to the internet or a library

Approximate time: 20 to 30 minutes per conversation

Cost: none

REPORT FROM THE FIELD

I completed this adventure on this date:

My adventure took place at:

I had help from the following people:

This adventure made me feel:

What I loved most about this adventure:

One thing I learned from this adventure:

One thing that surprised me about this adventure:

One thing I don't want to forget about this adventure:

── ADVENTURES ──
FOR YOUR HEALTH

"Believe you can and you're halfway there."

Theodore Roosevelt

It's never too early in life to think about taking care of your body. Taking care of your body can include thinking about what you're putting into your body, how you're moving your body, and how you're protecting your body (including your body's largest organ— your skin!) Some parts of these adventures are up to the people who take care of you—such as serving healthy meals or deciding to go on a nature hike. But YOU can take charge too when it comes to your health.

Here are several great adventures to do over and over again, especially if you're a kid who wants to be strong and healthy.

Run, Walk, Bike, or Scoot for a Cause

If you love being kind **and** you love to run or bike, this adventure's for you. Make your next run or bike ride more meaningful by signing up for a road race that raises awareness and funds for a cause that is important to you.

BONUS: You may find some lifelong friends in the process. Most road races have kids' fun runs and the best place to find those upcoming events in your city or state is ACTIVE.com. Not only is the race an adventure in itself but working with your family or friends to get ready for the big day is pretty darn fun too! Not into racing? Check out ACTIVEkids.com for more fun activities that are just perfect for kids.

→ **What You May Need to Complete this Adventure:**

Adult participation

Access to the internet to explore local run/walks in your community

Running shoes, a bike or scooter

Approximate time: practice a bit every day, with run/walk events typically lasting two to three hours (including the event day festivals)

Cost: none–$$

REPORT FROM THE FIELD

I completed this adventure on this date:

My adventure took place at:

I had help from the following people:

This adventure made me feel:

What I loved most about this adventure:

One thing I learned from this adventure:

One thing that surprised me about this adventure:

One thing I don't want to forget about this adventure:

Adventure 17
Drink More Water

When you're thirsty, cold water is the best thirst quencher. But did you know that if you're feeling thirsty, you might already be dehydrated? The trick is to drink water throughout the day, to make sure you're getting enough to keep your body strong and healthy.

⚡ First, track how many cups of water you drink on a normal day. Keep a record of your findings.

⚡ Then, do some research to find out how much water a kid your age should be drinking.

⚡ If you find you're drinking less than you should be, challenge yourself to drink the suggested amount of water for a week and see how it makes you feel.

BONUS: if you want to help your body **and** the planet, challenge yourself to bring a reusable water bottle everywhere you go—to school, sports, band, friends' houses, and everywhere in between. Not only will it support the good habit of drinking enough water, but you'll limit your use of single-use plastic water bottles.

➡ What You May Need to Complete this Adventure:

A reusable water bottle

Access to clean drinking water

Approximate time: one week, though this adventure can continue every day, forever!

Cost: none

REPORT FROM THE FIELD

I completed this adventure on this date:

My adventure took place at:

I had help from the following people:

This adventure made me feel:

What I loved most about this adventure:

One thing I learned from this adventure:

One thing that surprised me about this adventure:

One thing I don't want to forget about this adventure:

Take On a Family Fitness Adventure

Living healthy isn't just kind for your body, it can be a great activity for your family, too. This adventure involves lacing up your sneakers and going for a family hike. Before you stop reading, do **not** let the word "hike" scare you.

This adventure doesn't require big climbs, long distances, or super speed. It just requires getting out and moving. Start with a daily walk around your neighborhood or a weekend trek through whatever natural surroundings can be found in your community. Aim for one mile at first and track how you feel at the end of each hiking adventure. Can you keep it up for five days in a row? How about five weeks?

Challenge yourself to see how long you can keep this adventure going!

→ What You May Need to Complete this Adventure:

Family or friend to join you in the fitness adventure

Sneakers

Reusable water bottle

Approximate time: 20 minutes per day

Cost: none

FINISH

REPORT FROM THE FIELD

I completed this adventure on this date:

My adventure took place at:

I had help from the following people:

This adventure made me feel:

What I loved most about this adventure:

One thing I learned from this adventure:

One thing that surprised me about this adventure:

One thing I don't want to forget about this adventure:

Adventure 19

Try One New Fruit/Vegetable per Week for a Month

You may have a favorite food, but the best choice is to eat a lot of different foods and to always try new things. If you eat different foods, you're more likely to get the nutrients your body needs to grow strong and to stay healthy.

Go food shopping with your parents, grandparents, or guardians and walk through the produce aisle examining all the different fruits and vegetables that you've never tasted before. Consider trying at least one new type of fruit or vegetable each week, and help prepare it so you can learn more about it.

TiP! you should ***always*** aim for at least five servings of fruits and vegetables per day—two fruits and three vegetables.

Here's one combination that might work for you:

- ✫ At breakfast: ½ cup fruit (about four large strawberries, half of a sliced banana or a big handful of blueberries) on your cereal or a few leaves of spinach blended in with a morning fruit smoothie

- ✫ With lunch: six baby carrots or cucumber slices

- ✫ For a snack: an apple, celery slices with peanut butter, sliced red, green or orange peppers

- ✫ With dinner: ½ cup broccoli, asparagus, cauliflower or one cup of salad

Take part in preparing the vegetables, and you may find that you enjoy eating them even more!

Adult supervision

Access to grocery store or farmers market with a
wide selection of produce

Transportation, based on location of grocery store

Approximate time: one month

Cost: $ – $$

≥ health ≤

A NOTE FROM SOPHiA

When I completed this adventure with my family,
I tried a bunch of new vegetables like purple carrots
(we steamed them and added a little bit of honey before
serving), sweet potatoes (mashed!), sweet peppers and radishes
(in a green salad) and beets (roasted).

The sweet purple carrots were my favorite!

REPORT FROM THE FIELD

I completed this adventure on this date:

My adventure took place at:

I had help from the following people:

This adventure made me feel:

What I loved most about this adventure:

One thing I learned from this adventure:

One thing that surprised me about this adventure:

One thing I don't want to forget about this adventure:

Adventure 20

Learn at Least One New Active Sport Before this Year Is Over

One job you have as a kid—and it's a fun one—is that you get to figure out which activities you like best. Not everyone loves baseball or soccer. Maybe your passion is karate, kickball, or step dancing. The point is, there's no shortage of sports to learn, so why not take up a new one this year? Here's a list to get your mind thinking about what you'd like to learn:

Adventure Sports

- ⭐ canoeing
- ⭐ cross-country skiing
- ⭐ kayaking
- ⭐ rafting
- ⭐ surfing

Aquatic Sports

- ⭐ bodyboarding
- ⭐ diving
- ⭐ paddle boarding
- ⭐ rowing
- ⭐ snorkeling
- ⭐ swimming

Ball Sports

- ⭐ bowling
- ⭐ badminton
- ⭐ baseball
- ⭐ basketball
- ⭐ cricket
- ⭐ dodgeball
- ⭐ field hockey
- ⭐ football
- ⭐ golf
- ⭐ ice hockey
- ⭐ kickball
- ⭐ lacrosse
- ⭐ racquetball
- ⭐ rugby
- ⭐ soccer
- ⭐ softball
- ⭐ table tennis
- ⭐ tennis
- ⭐ volleyball

Extreme Sports

- ⭐ rock climbing
- ⭐ unicycling
- ⭐ skateboarding
- ⭐ snowboarding

Strength and Agility Sports

- ⭐ archery
- ⭐ baton twirling
- ⭐ cross-country running
- ⭐ cycling
- ⭐ dancing
- ⭐ horseback riding
- ⭐ fencing
- ⭐ figure skating
- ⭐ gymnastics
- ⭐ karate
- ⭐ mixed martial arts
- ⭐ trail running
- ⭐ tumbling

→ **What You May Need to Complete this Adventure:**

Sneakers

Access to the internet or a community recreation catalog to learn what sports are being offered in your area

Water bottle

Approximate time: one year or less

Cost: $ – $$$

A NOTE FROM SOPHiA:

I've tried out a bunch of great sports including baseball, mountain biking, rock climbing, field hockey, karate, paddle boarding, soccer, dance, and tennis. There's something I have loved about each one of them.

Baseball and field hockey are my favorites, but paddle boarding made for a great adventure with my family, and dance is a fun way to exercise my body while spending time with friends. I love trying new sports because they give me different ways to use and move my body.

WHAT ARE YOU GOING TO TRY?

REPORT FROM THE FIELD

I completed this adventure on this date:

My adventure took place at:

I had help from the following people:

This adventure made me feel:

What I loved most about this adventure:

One thing I learned from this adventure:

One thing that surprised me about this adventure:

One thing I don't want to forget about this adventure:

FOR OUR WORLD

> "Unless someone like you cares a whole awful lot, nothing is going to get better. It's not."
>
> Dr. Seuss

With pollution rates on the rise and climate change hurting our world and the species that live here, it's important for every kid to learn about nature and the ways we can protect and save it. For every eco-adventure you take on, you'll become more aware of the world around you and you'll better understand the consequences of climate change. Take on this next set of adventures knowing that you can play an important part in caring for our Earth and for our future.

Adventure 21
Limit Your Electricity Usage

Using less electricity in your home and at school is very kind for the environment. The less electricity we use, the less strain we put on an already overloaded energy grid. And the less we use, the less pollution is created to make that electricity.

There are plenty of ways to reduce your energy usage, from morning through night. Go on this energy-reducing adventure and know that you're playing a big part in caring for our planet.

☆ When you leave your bedroom each morning, make sure you turn off your lights.

☆ Love toast for breakfast? Make sure you unplug that toaster or other small appliances after each use. It may seem like energy isn't being used when that appliance isn't on, but electricity is still being used.

☆ Working with an adult, check the kinds of lightbulbs installed in your home. If you come across any incandescent lightbulbs (which produce a lot of heat and consume more electricity than any other type of bulb), consider swapping them out for eco-friendlier fluorescent, halogen, or LED bulbs.

☆ Take advantage of natural sunlight every chance you can. If you're doing homework or reading at home, sit near the sunny window rather than turning on all the lights.

☆ Resist lingering in front of the refrigerator with the door open. We get it—finding that perfect snack takes time. But every second the fridge door is open is another second of wasted energy. Pick out your snack with speed and close that fridge back up!

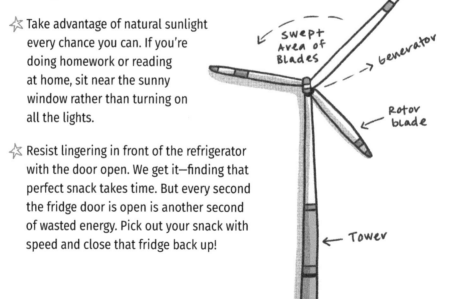

swept Area of Blades

→ Generator

Rotor blade

← Tower

DID YOU KNOW THAT ENERGY IS ALL AROUND YOU?

Energy sources can either be renewable or non-renewable.

Renewable energy is collected from renewable resources, such as natural sources or processes that are constantly replenished. Examples are solar (from the sun), wind, water, geothermal (from the earth) and biomass (from organic materials).

Non-renewable energy sources don't replenish, and were formed when prehistoric plants and animals died and were gradually buried by layers of soil and rock. The kind of fuel that was created varied depending on the conditions, like the kind of organic material (from plants or animals), how long it was buried, at what temperature, and under what pressure. Types of non-renewable energy are natural gas, coal and oil.

There are also lots of different kinds of energy, such as kinetic, thermal, and gravitational energy. Take this adventure a step further by reading more about various types of energy at energy.gov/science-innovation/energy-sources.

REPORT FROM THE FIELD

I completed this adventure on this date:

My adventure took place at:

I had help from the following people:

This adventure made me feel:

What I loved most about this adventure:

One thing I learned from this adventure:

One thing that surprised me about this adventure:

One thing I don't want to forget about this adventure:

Adventure 22
Take the Shower Time Challenge

Did you know that the average shower uses 2 ½ gallons of water per minute?[5] That's 25 gallons of water per ten minutes. That might not be Niagara Falls, but add together a country full of ten-minute showers and you're talking billions of gallons of water each day.

Saving water not only helps preserve our planet but it reduces the energy required to process and deliver water, which helps reduce pollution and conserve resources. Saving water now also means having water available in the future for recreational purposes, too.

For this adventure, start by timing your average shower for two to three days. Then, challenge yourself to cut down on your average shower time by one minute. The key to this adventure is to not go beyond ten minutes in total. Prefer baths over showers? No need to give up your bath completely. Consider swapping two of your weekly baths for showers each week, since they use much less water than baths.

Think you can do it—and still get all the shampoo out of your hair? We know you can!

→ **What You May Need to Complete this Adventure:**

Access to a shower

Approximate time: less than ten minutes per day

Cost: none

REPORT FROM THE FIELD

I completed this adventure on this date:

My adventure took place at:

I had help from the following people:

This adventure made me feel:

What I loved most about this adventure:

One thing I learned from this adventure:

One thing that surprised me about this adventure:

One thing I don't want to forget about this adventure:

Adventure 23
Create Habitat for Animals by Planting Native Wildflowers or Bushes

Have you ever examined the types of bushes or flowers that grow in your yard? They're very likely "native" to your neck of the woods, meaning that they're adapted to your local climate and soil conditions. Native plants and flowers are important because they provide nectar, pollen, and seeds that serve as food for native butterflies, insects, birds, and other animals. When non-native plants are introduced to an area, they have a lower likelihood of survival and they will often require pest control to survive.

Start this adventure by coming up with a list of ten plants that are local to your area. Then, ask your family if you can plant one of them around your house or apartment. We love butterflies, so we planted one of the many species of milkweed plant that is native to our home state of Maryland. We loved seeing caterpillars crawl along the leaves and lay their eggs, and we were able to watch the entire transformation process, from caterpillar to chrysalis to butterfly right from our kitchen window!

TIP! Not sure what plants are native to your area? We love this website, nwf.org/NativePlantFinder, which lets you search for native plants by zip code!

Want to take this adventure one step further? Work with your family, community group, club or school to organize a native planting day!

→ What You May Need to Complete this Adventure:

Adult supervision

Gardening gloves

Access to the internet or the library to do your research

Seeds of native plants and potting soil

Approximate time: one to three seasons (a growing cycle)

Cost: $$–$$$

A NOTE FROM SOPHIA:

My sister and I love helping our dad garden. It's a great outdoor adventure because we get to be surrounded by nature and we get to watch the progress of what we've planted over time. We also like making trips to the garden store, which is a great place to learn about plants and flowers that are native to our area. By focusing your gardening on native plants, you're being especially good to the animals and insects that live in your local environment.

REPORT FROM THE FIELD

I completed this adventure on this date:

My adventure took place at:

I had help from the following people:

This adventure made me feel:

What I loved most about this adventure:

One thing I learned from this adventure:

One thing that surprised me about this adventure:

One thing I don't want to forget about this adventure:

Adventure 24

Find at Least Three New Uses for Leftover Scraps of Paper

If you love arts and crafts as much as we do, then you probably have a nice little pile of scrap paper in your home. Rather than toss those scraps or put them right into the recycling bin, challenge yourself to re-use them.

☆ Cut them into small hearts or squares for pocket-sized thank you notes.

☆ Make a stack of gift tags for the next holiday season.

☆ Make confetti to adorn a birthday party table.

☆ Fold them down, then cut out corners and holes to make snowflakes that can adorn your windows.

☆ Cut out various shapes to dress up a photo album.

☆ Learn origami and make little gifts for your friends.

Have fun with this activity knowing that you're doing good for the planet **and** maybe also making someone's day!

➡️ **What You May Need to Complete this Adventure:**

Paper scraps

Pencil, pen or markers

Craft supplies such as stickers

Approximate time: ten minutes to one hour

Cost: none

REPORT FROM THE FIELD

I completed this adventure on this date:

My adventure took place at:

I had help from the following people:

This adventure made me feel:

What I loved most about this adventure:

One thing I learned from this adventure:

One thing that surprised me about this adventure:

One thing I don't want to forget about this adventure:

71

Adventure 25

Walk or Bike to All Nearby Locations

Just like conserving energy in your home is an important part in caring for our planet, so too is thinking about your personal carbon footprint.

How much is your family driving each week, and can you replace any of those drives with different forms of transportation, such as walking or biking? This one's not always possible, depending on where you live, but if you find that your family relies on the car for daily trips down to the local grocery store or market, consider suggesting that you condense those four or five trips a week into two, or that you walk or bike to the market one day instead of driving.

TIP! If you're close enough, consider walking or biking to school once per week.

→ What You May Need to Complete this Adventure:

Sneakers or a bike

Bike helmet

Approximate time: dependent on destination

Cost: none

REPORT FROM THE FIELD

I completed this adventure on this date:

My adventure took place at:

I had help from the following people:

This adventure made me feel:

What I loved most about this adventure:

One thing I learned from this adventure:

One thing that surprised me about this adventure:

One thing I don't want to forget about this adventure:

73

Adventure 26
Support Local Farmers

We love walking to the small farm stand near our home, which is usually set up between June and September. It's fun to talk with the farmers about what they're growing, to learn more about how that season's weather is affecting their crops, and to know that we're supporting that local farm. If you live in a place that offers farmers markets or farm stands, start this adventure off with a visit and replace one fruit or vegetable that you would have purchased from the grocery store with something that was grown by a local farmer.

If you don't have any farm stands or farms near you, explore the options to have local produce delivered to your home. Most communities provide co-op services to support local farmers and there are also plenty of subscription services that help distribute less-than-perfect (but still delicious) produce, such as those funny-shaped but still delicious apples or cucumbers that grocery stores won't often sell, right to your door for a discounted cost. Some of our favorite services include:

- ☆ ImperfectFoods.com
- ☆ HungryHarvest.net
- ☆ MisfitsMarket.com

→ What You May Need to Complete this Adventure:

Adult supervision

Access to transportation (if farm or farmers market is not within walking distance)

Approximate time: one to two hours

Cost: $–$$

REPORT FROM THE FIELD

I completed this adventure on this date:

My adventure took place at:

I had help from the following people:

This adventure made me feel:

What I loved most about this adventure:

One thing I learned from this adventure:

One thing that surprised me about this adventure:

One thing I don't want to forget about this adventure:

Make Homemade Bird Feeders

If you think it's nice hearing the birds chirp outside your window each morning, this next adventure's for you. Making homemade bird feeders is a fun way to get to know which birds are native to your area and a great way to help little winged friends when their food sources are scarce in the wintertime. This adventure's good for the environment too, as bird feeders can be made using all-natural items from your yard or recycle bin.

Here are some ideas for homemade bird feeders:

⭐ **Upcycle an old teacup and saucer set.** Start by sanding down the bottom of the cup and the center of the saucers. Then apply a strong adhesive glue to attach the pieces together. Once the teacup and saucer are firmly affixed, use a hot glue gun to attach the bird feeder to a two- to three-foot wooden dowel (which you can find at your local hardware store) Plant the dowel in your yard and add some bird seed. That's all there is to it!

⭐ **Use basic pantry staples.** This simple bird feeder only requires three pipe cleaners and a few handfuls of Cheerios®, as well as some yarn or string to hang the bird feeder in your yard. To make this bird feeder, thread the Cheerios onto two of your three pipe cleaners. Leave a bit of space at the end of each pipe cleaner so you can twist the ends together, making a circle of Cheerios. Then, take your third pipe cleaner, also string it with Cheerios, and lay it across the center of the circle, twisting the ends around the gaps in the circle where our first two pipe cleaners were joined. The third pipe cleaner serves as the perch for small birds to sit on. Tie a 1 ½-foot piece of yarn to each end of the third pipe cleaner so you can hang your cool new bird feeder from a tree.

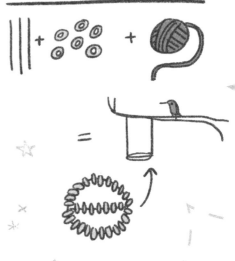

PANTRY BIRD FEEDER

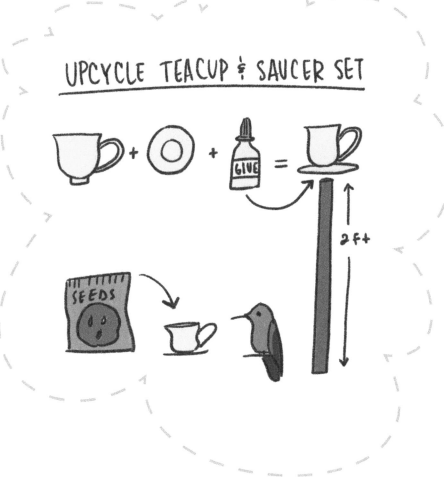

→ **What You May Need to Complete this Adventure:**

Adult supervision

Bird seed and bird feeder supplies, as noted above

Approximate time: one hour or less

Cost: none – $

UPCYCLE TEACUP & SAUCER SET

SEEDS

GLUE

2 ft

REPORT FROM THE FIELD

I completed this adventure on this date:

My adventure took place at:

I had help from the following people:

This adventure made me feel:

What I loved most about this adventure:

One thing I learned from this adventure:

One thing that surprised me about this adventure:

One thing I don't want to forget about this adventure:

Adventure 28
Go Meatless At Least One Meal Per Week

Did you know that it takes approximately 1,700 gallons of water to produce a single pound of beef, versus 39 gallons of water to produce an equal pound of vegetables?[6] That cheeseburger might taste great, but there's a lot of kindness—for you and the environment—if you just cut out meat from your diet once per week.

Not only can going meatless reduce your carbon footprint, but it can reduce your risk of chronic preventable conditions such as cardiovascular disease, diabetes and obesity.

Go meatless and you'll find that you have something special in common with some of the world's most elite athletes, such as tennis pro Venus Williams, Formula One racing star Lewis Hamilton, pro football player Colin Kaepernick, and basketball star Kyrie Irving—who have all removed meat from their diets.

TIP! Learn more, get recipes, and take the Meatless Monday pledge at MeatlessMonday.com, or try one of our favorite kid-friendly vegetarian recipes at veggie-kids.com.

→ meat

→ What You May Need to Complete this Adventure:

Adult supervision

Access to a kitchen

Access to the internet or a cookbook

Approximate time: one hour or less

Cost: $-$$

DID YOU KNOW THAT PRODUCING BEEF...

uses 20 times the land and emits 20 times the emissions as growing beans, AND requires more than ten times more resources than producing chicken?[7] That's because cows, lambs, and goats all release methane—a greenhouse gas many times more potent than carbon.

REPORT FROM THE FIELD

I completed this adventure on this date:

My adventure took place at:

I had help from the following people:

This adventure made me feel:

What I loved most about this adventure:

One thing I learned from this adventure:

One thing that surprised me about this adventure:

One thing I don't want to forget about this adventure:

Adventure 29
Go on a Nature Walk

A nature walk is a fun and easy way to be kind to the planet. Get yourself a magnifying glass and a little notebook and pencil to get this adventure going. First, take a walk around the perimeter of your home or neighborhood. Notice the kinds of plants, flowers, rocks, and soil that exist there. Then, take a second lap, looking even closer under the leaves to examine the insects, soil, and animals that live in the area. Get down on your hands and knees and look closely. You'll be amazed how much there is to find in every square of nature.

Speaking of squares, we **love** the series of books called *One Small Square* by Donald Silver and Patricia Wynne. It's the perfect companion for helping you to discover all the magic that's living right under your nose.

There's just one rule for this adventure: If you see anything that doesn't belong, such as food wrappers or discarded items, pick them up and dispose of them—and be sure not to add to the litter along the way. The key to a good nature walk is to **leave no trace** of your visit, which means that you don't leave any trash or items behind.

➡️ **What You May Need to Complete this Adventure:**

Sneakers

Microscope or binoculars

Approximate time: 20 minutes to two hours

Cost: none–$ (based on location of nature walk)

foot prints

REPORT FROM THE FIELD

I completed this adventure on this date:

My adventure took place at:

I had help from the following people:

This adventure made me feel:

What I loved most about this adventure:

One thing I learned from this adventure:

One thing that surprised me about this adventure:

One thing I don't want to forget about this adventure:

— ADVENTURES —

FOR YOUR MIND

"Always try to be a little kinder than necessary."

J.M. Barrie

Have you ever had a day when you felt stressed or overwhelmed? That can be a tough feeling to shake, especially if you don't have a loved one nearby to comfort you. Many kids deal with the everyday stress of not having enough to eat, not having access to education, and maybe not even feeling safe at home. It's important every day to find time to care for others, just as much as you're finding time to care for yourself. This set of adventures is designed to expand your mind, which is often one of the best ways to care for your mind.

Adventure 30
Start a Little Free Library in Your Neighborhood

There's nothing better than getting lost in a great book, except maybe sharing that book with a friend. Sharing the love of reading with someone else is one of our favorite adventures in kindness, and now there's a movement underway to share that love even farther and wider with your community.

For this adventure, we invite you to join the world's largest book sharing movement by building a Little Free Library in front of your home or in your community so that everyone can share in a love of books. There are now more than 100,000 Little Free Libraries across the world, and if your community doesn't yet have one, this would be a great adventure for you, your family or school to take on together.

TIP! Learn more, including how to build and stock your Little Free Library at LittleFreeLibrary.org.

➡ **What You May Need to Complete this Adventure:**

Access to books at home or at the library

Approximate time: one week or less

Cost: none–$

REPORT FROM THE FIELD

I completed this adventure on this date:

My adventure took place at:

I had help from the following people:

This adventure made me feel:

What I loved most about this adventure:

One thing I learned from this adventure:

One thing that surprised me about this adventure:

One thing I don't want to forget about this adventure:

Write a Letter to the Author of Your Favorite Book

There's nothing more special than telling someone how much they mean to you. If there's a book that you just love or a book that you hoped would never end, write a letter to that author and tell them how their book made you feel.

You can usually find the mailing or email address for your author in the front or back of the book, alongside the name of the publishing company. If that doesn't work, you can email the publisher and ask if they can pass your letter on to the author.

→ **What You May Need to Complete this Adventure:**

Notecard, envelope and a stamp

Approximate time: one hour or less

Cost: none – $

REPORT FROM THE FIELD

I completed this adventure on this date:

My adventure took place at:

I had help from the following people:

This adventure made me feel:

What I loved most about this adventure:

One thing I learned from this adventure:

One thing that surprised me about this adventure:

One thing I don't want to forget about this adventure:

Adventure 32

Organize a Book Swap at Your School or in Your Community

Take your love of reading to a whole new level by organizing a book swap with your neighborhood friends or school. Start by collecting a handful of books that you've already enjoyed and ask your friends or classmates to do the same. Set up the swap in one of your homes, your school, or your community center. For each book someone contributes to the book swap, provide them one ticket in return to use towards a fresh book.

Collect any donated or leftover books to bring to a local school or homeless shelter.

➡ What You May Need to Complete this Adventure:

The participation of friends or family members

A collection of gently-used books

Access to a school, community room, or home to set up the book swap

Approximate time: one day to one week

Cost: none–$

REPORT FROM THE FIELD

I completed this adventure on this date:

My adventure took place at:

I had help from the following people:

This adventure made me feel:

What I loved most about this adventure:

One thing I learned from this adventure:

One thing that surprised me about this adventure:

One thing I don't want to forget about this adventure:

Participate in Election Day

You may be too young to cast a vote, but you're not too young to care about the election process. Having a say in how your government is run is an incredibly powerful thing and an opportunity you should never waste.

Here in the United States, every citizen over the age of 18 has the right to vote, but that isn't the case in every country and it wasn't the case in the U.S. until recently. Did you know that women didn't gain the right to vote until 1920 and many African American, Latino, Asian American, and Native American women didn't get the right to vote until the 1960s?[8] That means a lot of group decisions about issues that affected all members of a community were made without the whole group being involved.

Here are a few ideas to get you started:

⭐ Use your community's next election, whether it be a local election or a presidential election, to learn about the candidates, understand what they stand for, and witness the voting process firsthand.

⭐ Read the promotional postcards and mailings that get delivered from various candidates to your home and learn where these candidates stand on the issues.

⭐ Watch a debate or attend a local town hall meeting to hear the candidates present their ideas.

⭐ Ask if you can go with your parents, grandparents or another caring adult to the voting booth.

Every experience you get with the election day process will make you more ready when it is your turn.

Adult participation

Access to your town's election ballot
(this is usually mailed home a few weeks before election day),
for some pre-reading and discussion

Approximate time: 20 minutes to two weeks

Cost: none

DID YOU KNOW THAT IN THE U.S...

Voter turnout—the percentage of qualified voters who vote—often depends on the type of election being held.

More people tend to vote in presidential elections than in other elections. Even in this case, though, many people who are qualified to vote do not. In the 2000 presidential election, for example, only 51 percent of the electorate (all qualified voters) turned out.[9]

REPORT FROM THE FIELD

I completed this adventure on this date:

My adventure took place at:

I had help from the following people:

This adventure made me feel:

What I loved most about this adventure:

One thing I learned from this adventure:

One thing that surprised me about this adventure:

One thing I don't want to forget about this adventure:

Learn How to Calculate a Generous Tip

Did you know that you can use your awesome math skills to be kind? It's common to struggle with how much to tip someone, whether it be the pizza delivery person or the barber. Years ago, the standard tip was ten percent of the total cost, but more recently the average tip ranges between 15 percent and 20 percent.

Even if you're not paying the bill, use every service experience as an opportunity to help calculate a generous tip. Start by calculating ten percent of the bill and then double that amount for a 20 percent tip. To calculate a ten percent tip, take the total bill and simply move the decimal point from wherever it is one space to the left.

Here's an example: a ten percent gratuity on a $15.00 bill would be $1.50. Doubling the ten percent tip would provide the correct amount for a 20 percent tip ($3.00). Below are some standard tip amounts to help calculate appropriate costs.

✬ Delivery person (including pizza): 10%, $2.00 minimum

✬ Waiter/waitress: 20%

✬ Cab driver: 10%, $2.00–$5.00 minimum

✬ Barber/hairstylist: 15% minimum, though most recommend closer to 25%

Try out the worksheet on the next page and in no time, you'll be calculating generous tips like a pro.

$$\begin{array}{r} \$50.00 \\ \times\ .20 \\ \hline 10.00 \end{array}$$

$5 + 5 = x$

π

$a^2 + b^2 = c^2$

Adult participation

Access to the bill at the end of your next restaurant meal, haircut, or food delivery

Approximate time: one hour or less

Cost: no cost needed to practice, $–$$ in tip money depending on the total cost of the service provided

PRACTICE SPACE TO CALCULATE TIP AMOUNTS:

bill amount	10%	20%
$10.00	$1.00	$2.00
$25.00		
$17.50		
$56.35		
$89.00		

REPORT FROM THE FIELD

I completed this adventure on this date:

My adventure took place at:

I had help from the following people:

This adventure made me feel:

What I loved most about this adventure:

One thing I learned from this adventure:

One thing that surprised me about this adventure:

One thing I don't want to forget about this adventure:

Learn to Say Hello in 35 Different Languages

Hello. Hi. Hey. Hiya.

The simple act of saying hello to someone in their native language is not only a kind gesture, but also a great sign of respect. And, since you've probably already mastered the many types of greetings in your native language, use this adventure to learn how to say "Hello" in several other languages.

By expanding the languages you speak, rather than limiting yourself to one single language, you'll be far more able to connect with those in your community who speak different languages. Learning a language is no fun if you can't use it, so try out your new words on your friends and family.

TIP! Check out the guide at the end of the book to help you learn 35 different ways to say Hello.

BONUS: Take this adventure one step further by exploring the locations of each of the featured countries on a map!

→ **What You May Need to Complete this Adventure:**

Just yourself, and access to a world map if you decide to complete the bonus adventure

Approximate time: one week to one month

Cost: none – $

REPORT FROM THE FIELD

I completed this adventure on this date:

My adventure took place at:

I had help from the following people:

This adventure made me feel:

What I loved most about this adventure:

One thing I learned from this adventure:

One thing that surprised me about this adventure:

One thing I don't want to forget about this adventure:

Adventure 36
Expand Your Reading List

We love reading because of how much it opens our minds to new ideas and different cultures. But we also know how many books default to old stereotypes such as the white knight or the princess who needs saving.

If you're ready for more diverse views of our world, head to your local library and take on one or more of the following reading challenges:

☆ Find at least five books that involve characters who break commonly held beliefs or assumptions, such as girls or persons of color in lead character roles, or as the heroes and heroines of the story.

☆ Find at least five books with main characters who live in countries different from your own.

☆ Find at least five books with main characters who have a different religion from your own.

☆ Find at least five books, each with main characters of a different age, and all showing courage, independence or strength.

TIP! Check out page 148 of this book for a great list of books that teach empathy and kindness

→ **What You May Need to Complete this Adventure:**

Adult participation

Access to the library, a local bookstore, or the internet

Approximate time: one week or less

Cost: none – $

REPORT FROM THE FIELD

I completed this adventure on this date:

My adventure took place at:

I had help from the following people:

This adventure made me feel:

What I loved most about this adventure:

One thing I learned from this adventure:

One thing that surprised me about this adventure:

One thing I don't want to forget about this adventure:

FOR YOUR COMMUNITY

"No act of kindness, no matter how small, is ever wasted."

Aesop

A strong, vibrant community thrives on the participation of every resident, no matter their age or position in the community. When every person chooses to participate in the community—whether by voting, attending community meetings and events, supporting local businesses, or taking part in volunteer projects that support and celebrate the community—everyone wins, and the place you live becomes a place where everyone feels they belong. The adventures in this section are designed to help you explore and learn more about your community, while creating ways for you to support, strengthen, and celebrate the place you live.

Adventure 37
Smile, Don't Stare

If you've ever come across someone in a wheelchair or with special needs and found yourself wondering what "happened" to that person, you wouldn't be alone. It's a natural human reflex to stare when you see someone who looks different from you. But that doesn't mean it's the right thing to do. Have you ever thought about how hurtful those stares might be to the person on the other end? Truth is, it's okay to look, but it's even better to ask a question. And it's best in every case to turn that stare into a smile.

Our friends at the Lollipop Kids Foundation (lollipopkidsfoundation.org) started a campaign in 2014 designed to remind people to smile, not stare when they come across someone living with a disability. Rather than make a differently-abled person feel isolated, consider how you can lead with kindness. Often, it need not be more than a simple smile. Challenge yourself to stop yourself before the stare starts and replace it with a smile.

➡️ **What You May Need to Complete this Adventure:**

Approximate time: just a few minutes each day can make a difference

Cost: none

REPORT FROM THE FIELD

I completed this adventure on this date:

My adventure took place at:

I had help from the following people:

This adventure made me feel:

What I loved most about this adventure:

One thing I learned from this adventure:

One thing that surprised me about this adventure:

One thing I don't want to forget about this adventure:

Interview an Older Neighbor About Their Life Experiences

Have you ever felt lonely? For many aging adults—who may not have friends or family living nearby, or who may no longer drive—this is a very common feeling, and it's often referred to as social isolation. Some reports note that close to 50 percent of older adults experience social isolation, which can lead to a greater number of falls and broken bones, hospitalizations and many other health issues. But, by every account, a sense of community can reduce the feeling of social isolation.

To help with this problem, we invite you to talk with an older person and interview them. Choose a person at least 65 years old. Ask questions about your subject's experiences as a child, as a young adult, and as an older adult. Record the interview using a journal or an audio recorder to make sure you capture everything that your subject shares, and then write or type up your interview. Give them a copy when you're done—they probably would like it written down!

Not only is this a great way to learn about people who have lived experiences different from your own, but it's a kind gesture for someone who might live alone and may not have as many chances to socialize with family and friends. Here are some questions that might help to guide your interview:

- ☆ Where did you live as a child?
  Tell me about your family and your home.
  What was your neighborhood like?

- ☆ Did you have pets as a child?
  If so, what kind and what were their names?

- ☆ Did you have a nickname as a child?
  How did you get it?

☆ What was your favorite subject in school? Was homework hard or easy for you?

☆ Can you remember a historic event that happened when you were young? How did that event affect you?

☆ What was your first job?

☆ Did you take family trips? Which one stands out as being among your favorite?

☆ What kinds of games or sports did you play?

☆ What are some of the biggest changes you've seen in our country in your lifetime?

☆ What age or age range has been your favorite thus far?

After the interview concludes, write a note to your subject, thanking them for their time. Then, reflect on the following questions:

☆ What was the interview like?

☆ What are the most important things you learned about your older friend or family member?

☆ What similar experiences have you had?

→ **What You May Need to Complete this Adventure:**

The participation of an older neighbor or family member

A notebook and pen or an audio recorder

A notecard and stamp for your thank you note

Approximate time: one week or less

REPORT FROM THE FIELD

I completed this adventure on this date:

My adventure took place at:

I had help from the following people:

This adventure made me feel:

What I loved most about this adventure:

One thing I learned from this adventure:

One thing that surprised me about this adventure:

One thing I don't want to forget about this adventure:

Adventure 39

Put Together Care Kits for People Experiencing Homelessness

Have you ever wondered where your next meal would be coming from, or have you ever been without a bathroom to brush your teeth, take a shower, or change into clean clothes? For people experiencing homelessness, these questions are a daily part of life.

But the good news is that you can play an important role in caring for someone experiencing homelessness.

There are several different routes you can take with your DIY homeless care packages. You should aim to keep it light as the recipient will likely have to carry it around with them. It's also a good idea to try to make the bag something that can be reused, such as a small water-resistant grocery bag that can be folded up and tucked away.

There are three basic needs that you can try to cover with your bag:

☆ Protection from the elements (cold and hot)

☆ Hygiene

☆ Nutrition

Putting together homeless care packages is a great way to make a difference in your community and they can make a big impact on the life of another person. To distribute the bags, you can reach out to a local homeless shelter, carry a few of them with you, or tuck a few inside your family's car, so you have them ready if people need them.

If you are struggling with what to put in a homeless care package, these are some great options:

- ⭐ Weather protection
- ⭐ Sunscreen
- ⭐ Hot Hands® for hands and feet
- ⭐ Emergency blankets
- ⭐ Ponchos
- ⭐ Lip balm (e.g., Chapstick®)
- ⭐ Socks

- ⭐ First aid kit
- ⭐ Food
- ⭐ Fruit cocktail
- ⭐ Raisins
- ⭐ Water
- ⭐ Slim Jim®
- ⭐ Chicken or tuna salad

Be aware that some people might not want to accept your care kit and that's okay too. You can't always control how someone else uses your gift, but you can always act with kindness.

➡️ **What You May Need to Complete this Adventure:**

Adult supervision

Reusable plastic bags

Care kit supplies, such as those listed above

Approximate time: one week or less, but can be done on an ongoing basis

Cost: $–$$

REPORT FROM THE FIELD

I completed this adventure on this date:

My adventure took place at:

I had help from the following people:

This adventure made me feel:

What I loved most about this adventure:

One thing I learned from this adventure:

One thing that surprised me about this adventure:

One thing I don't want to forget about this adventure:

Adventure 40
Pay It Forward

In the movie *Pay It Forward*, a 7th grader named Trevor is given the following assignment by his social studies teacher: "Think of an idea to change our world—and put it into action!" Trevor comes up with the idea of paying it forward: you do a big favor for three different people and tell each of them not to pay you back, but to pay it forward to three other people who, in turn, each pay it forward to three more.

Go ahead and pay it forward to three people who need help and tell them not to pay you back, but to make a commitment to help three other people when they can. Here are a few ideas to get you started:

☆ Pull up the garbage cans or recycling bins for a neighbor on trash day.

☆ Hold the elevator for a family with small children.

☆ Share your umbrella when it next rains with someone who's walking without one.

☆ If you see someone taking pictures of their family, offer to take the picture so that this person can be alongside their family in the photo.

☆ Help an older neighbor by mowing their lawn, watering their flower bed, or getting their groceries out of the car and into their home.

➡ **What You May Need to Complete this Adventure:**

Just you and your kind self

Approximate time: a few minutes each day

Cost: none

REPORT FROM THE FIELD

I completed this adventure on this date:

My adventure took place at:

I had help from the following people:

This adventure made me feel:

What I loved most about this adventure:

One thing I learned from this adventure:

One thing that surprised me about this adventure:

One thing I don't want to forget about this adventure:

Find Ten Locally-Owned Businesses and Support Them

Small businesses are often the heart of a community, but they must compete with much larger, more established businesses.

One of the best ways to support small businesses is to go shopping! See what's sprouting at the local farmers market or buy some flowers for your teacher at the local flower shop.

Not able to go shopping? Then find ways to help spread the word about the small businesses in your town. Is there a new ice cream shop or bakery nearby? Offer to help spread the word by posting flyers or distributing coupons. Another great way to complete this adventure is to simply visit each one of your identified small businesses and say thank you.

Small businesses create new jobs, provide personal experiences, and support your local economy. When they do well, your whole community does well.

➡️ **What You May Need to Complete this Adventure:**

Adult supervision

Transportation

Approximate time: one month or less, but can be done on an ongoing basis

Cost: none−$$$

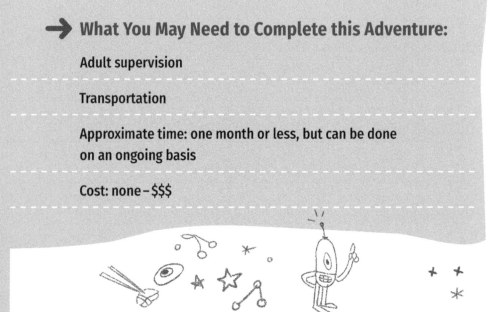

REPORT FROM THE FIELD

I completed this adventure on this date:

My adventure took place at:

I had help from the following people:

This adventure made me feel:

What I loved most about this adventure:

One thing I learned from this adventure:

One thing that surprised me about this adventure:

One thing I don't want to forget about this adventure:

Adventure 42

Take the "Day in a Wheelchair" Challenge

Have you ever experienced walking on crutches or moving about in a wheelchair? If so, you're probably aware of how difficult it can be for people who are physically challenged to get around town. It's tough to access certain areas without ramps and difficult to find wheelchair accessible bathrooms.

For this adventure, take one day making note of all the places you go and how your daily motions might change if you were in a wheelchair. Take notice of how often you rely on stairs, where the nearest elevators or ramps are located, and even the quality of city streets and sidewalks (cracks and bumps are hard to roll over).

Individuals living with physical challenges often have their needs ignored because able-bodied people just don't see or experience the world in the same way. Take the time to understand if accessibility is a challenge in your community, and then think about what you might be able to do to help. Don't underestimate your ability to advocate for improved sidewalks, safer crosswalks, more ramps, or more accessible bathroom facilities.

➡ What You May Need to Complete this Adventure:

A notebook and pen

Approximate time: one day

Cost: none

REPORT FROM THE FIELD

I completed this adventure on this date:

My adventure took place at:

I had help from the following people:

This adventure made me feel:

What I loved most about this adventure:

One thing I learned from this adventure:

One thing that surprised me about this adventure:

One thing I don't want to forget about this adventure:

Email One of Your Elected Officials About a Political Topic

Do you know the names of the people in charge of your local government?

If not, then let's start this adventure by researching the names of your elected representatives. Find out who your senators and congresspeople are, as well as your mayor, governor, and local, county, or city representatives.

Once you've completed that research, consider taking your civic responsibility to the next level by researching the issues that each elected official is actively working on, and what issues they seem to care about most. You can hop online with an adult or head over to the library to do this research.

Once you've found the issues that each of your representatives is working on, write a letter to at least one of them, with a question or feedback about how you think they're doing. Elected officials need to hear from their community and the voices of kids are especially important to them. Remember, voting is not the only way you can get involved in the political system. Consider all the ways to use your voice to help advocate for the issues that matter most to you, such as letter writing, and speaking out on topics that are important to you.

And remember this: a handwritten note from a child can be more powerful than a hundred email messages from adults.

➡️ **What You May Need to Complete this Adventure:**

Access to the library or internet to research your issue

Approximate time: one week or less, but can be done on an ongoing basis

Cost: none

REPORT FROM THE FIELD

I completed this adventure on this date:

My adventure took place at:

I had help from the following people:

This adventure made me feel:

What I loved most about this adventure:

One thing I learned from this adventure:

One thing that surprised me about this adventure:

One thing I don't want to forget about this adventure:

Write Down What You Would Do If You Were Mayor for a Day

Have you ever thought what it would be like to be in control of the decisions that govern your community? What would you change? How would you go about hearing people's concerns and then addressing them?

Setting aside any visions of free ice cream every day, what would you do if you were mayor of your city? Just as you did in Adventure #13 (Ideal World), and maybe also in Adventure #43 (researching and letter writing your elected official) think about what's **not** working in your city, town, or community, and what you could do to change it. How would you go about it, and who would you need to help you make change happen?

Then, once you've done your thinking, write or email your local representatives with your ideas.

→ **What You May Need to Complete this Adventure:**

Access to the library or internet to research your city's issue

Approximate time: one week or less, but can be done on an ongoing basis

Cost: none

A NOTE FROM SOPHIA:

I loved doing this adventure with my fourth grade class. Some tips from my experience: Learn about what your town's mayor does, and what they are focused on this year. Then, think of what you could do to improve your community if you were in your mayor's shoes. What would make your town happier, healthier, or safer?

REPORT FROM THE FIELD

I completed this adventure on this date:

My adventure took place at:

I had help from the following people:

This adventure made me feel:

What I loved most about this adventure:

One thing I learned from this adventure:

One thing that surprised me about this adventure:

One thing I don't want to forget about this adventure:

ADVENTURES
FOR YOUR SCHOOL

"Let us remember one book, one pen, and one teacher can change the world."

Malala Yousafzai

In our home, we talk a lot about investing in the things that are worth protecting. By investing, we don't always mean with money, but with our time, attention, and care. Education is usually at the top of our list. Did you ever stop to think just how much time you spend in your school building? You spend more time there than anywhere else as a kid and it should be a place where you feel happy, inspired, and excited to learn. It should also be a place where everyone feels like they belong, and where everyone has access to nutritious food, good books, and supportive friends and teachers. This set of adventures is designed to help you invest in things worth protecting, such as your school community.

Create a Recycling Initiative

Much of what we buy, such as food, bottled water, or individually wrapped snacks, is either packaged in or made of plastic that we discard after a single use. This waste accounts for nearly half of all plastic waste worldwide. And if we don't do anything to change how we use and dispose of plastic, the world's oceans are projected to contain more plastic than fish by weight by the year 2050.[10] (Flip back to Adventure #2 to learn more on this topic.)

Here's the good news: **you** can take action to eliminate using single-use plastics today! Is your school still using plastic cutlery in the cafeteria or straws in their milk containers? Are your lunch snacks packaged in individual plastic bags? Do you use a plastic water bottle and immediately toss it in the trash?

For this adventure, consider how you can help cut down on single use plastics, and advocate in your school for more sustainable options such as paper straws, recycled plates, or reusable cutlery.

➡️ **What You May Need to Complete This Adventure:**

School or adult supervision

Approximate time: one month or less, but can be done on an ongoing basis

Cost: none

REPORT FROM THE FIELD

I completed this adventure on this date:

My adventure took place at:

I had help from the following people:

This adventure made me feel:

What I loved most about this adventure:

One thing I learned from this adventure:

One thing that surprised me about this adventure:

One thing I don't want to forget about this adventure:

Adventure 46

Spread Joy with Kindness Rocks

Would you like to spread happiness around like sunshine? This is a simple adventure that can do just that! Start by heading outside and collecting some small, smooth rocks from around your yard or neighborhood. Wash and dry them well and then cover them with a full coat of paint.

When the paint has dried, use a separate paint color or marker to add words of happiness and encouragement to each rock, such as "you are loved," "kindness rocks," "today's the day," "stay positive," or "be brave."

Once the rocks are ready, deliver them to people in and around your school: teachers, bus drivers, school counselors and friends. You can either leave them in places where your friends and family will find them or give them directly as gifts. Either way, know that you'll be spreading sunshine to anyone on the receiving end.

➜ What You May Need to Complete This Adventure:

Small rocks, collected from around your yard or neighborhood

Water-based paint and a paintbrush or markers

Approximate time: one hour or less

Cost: none – $

REPORT FROM THE FIELD

I completed this adventure on this date:

My adventure took place at:

I had help from the following people:

This adventure made me feel:

What I loved most about this adventure:

One thing I learned from this adventure:

One thing that surprised me about this adventure:

One thing I don't want to forget about this adventure:

Adventure 47
Organize an Old Bike Drive

Do you have an old bike that you've grown too big for, tucked away in your garage, but still in good shape? Did you know that instead of collecting spiderwebs, it can provide transportation for kids and adults living in under-resourced communities in the U.S. and across the globe so that they can get to school or go to work? Yep, your unused bike can change someone's life.

Organizing a bike drive for a local community organization or a global program such as Bikes for the World (bikesfortheworld.org/get-involved/how-to-organize-a-collection) is a great way to engage your community and support families in villages around the world. By helping find under-used bikes in your neighborhood, you are impacting our local environment (let's keep these bikes out of the landfills) and improving lives thousands of miles from home.

➡️ **What You May Need to Complete This Adventure:**

School or adult participation

Art supplies to create flyers and posters

Approximate time: one month or less

Cost: $–$$

A NOTE FROM SOPHiA

I remember handing down my first bike to my little sister and how much she loved getting it. When we grow out of our bikes, we plan to pass our fun of riding bikes on to someone else who doesn't yet have a bike.

REPORT FROM THE FIELD

I completed this adventure on this date:

My adventure took place at:

I had help from the following people:

This adventure made me feel:

What I loved most about this adventure:

One thing I learned from this adventure:

One thing that surprised me about this adventure:

One thing I don't want to forget about this adventure:

Host a Mix It Up at Lunch Day

How often do you sit with the same group of friends at the lunch table? If you haven't mixed it up in a while, maybe now's the time. Mix it Up at Lunch Day is an international campaign that encourages students to break out of our "comfort zones" to explore new ways of getting to know the people around us. Schools can register to host a Mix It Up event on any day of the year and use the resources found on www.tolerance.org/mix-it-up to make the day even better.

This adventure is about much more than just sitting next to another friend at lunch. The reason many kids get teased, bullied, or picked on is because they are somehow seen as different—in the way they look, dress, or talk, or even the family they come from. Sometimes it may feel scary to make friends with someone who seems very different from you. But you may find out some cool things you never would have learned if you always stuck with people just like you. Your new friend's family may come from a different country than yours, or their parents might not have the same genders as yours, for instance, but they may love some of the same games, movies, books, or TV shows that you do.

Bring the idea for a Mix it Up at Lunch Day to your student government or school principal to get support for the idea.

TiP! You can register, see if your school is registered and download free resources at tolerance.org/mix-it-up .

➡ What You May Need to Complete This Adventure:

School or adult participation

Approximate time: one month or less

Cost: none

REPORT FROM THE FIELD

I completed this adventure on this date:

My adventure took place at:

I had help from the following people:

This adventure made me feel:

What I loved most about this adventure:

One thing I learned from this adventure:

One thing that surprised me about this adventure:

One thing I don't want to forget about this adventure:

Make Bookmarks for Your Classmates and Teacher

This Valentine's Day consider skipping the candy and make bookmarks for each of your classmates instead. Not only is it a healthier option, but it's a practical tool that shows off your creative side and tells your friends how much you care about them. (This adventure also helps you complete Adventure #24—finding new uses for old scrap paper!)

Experiment with different designs, and consider personalizing the bookmarks with your classmates' names, or including a great quote about reading, such as one of the sayings included below:

☆ *"You can find magic wherever you look. Sit back and relax. All you need is a book."* **Dr. Seuss**

☆ *"Home is wherever my books are."* **Kerstin Gier**

☆ *"Reading is dreaming with eyes open."* **Anissa Trisdianty**

☆ *"A book is a dream that you hold in your hands."* **Neil Gaiman**

➡ **What You May Need to Complete This Adventure:**

Paper and craft supplies

Approximate time: one day

Cost: none–$

REPORT FROM THE FIELD

I completed this adventure on this date:

My adventure took place at:

I had help from the following people:

This adventure made me feel:

What I loved most about this adventure:

One thing I learned from this adventure:

One thing that surprised me about this adventure:

One thing I don't want to forget about this adventure:

133

FOR THE TROOPS

> "A single act of kindness throws out roots in all directions, and the roots spring up and make new trees."
>
> Amelia Earhart

"Support Our Troops" is a popular slogan, and one that you've probably seen on the bumper of cars or trucks in the form of a magnetic ribbon or sticker. But really supporting our troops—the people of our military who sacrifice their own personal freedoms and time with their families to defend our country—requires a lot more than posting a bumper sticker or magnet. The following adventures are designed for you to support members of the military in your community and around the globe. In the process, you may learn a lot more about your country, too.

Interview a Service Member

Whether you're passing by a uniformed service member in the airport, the crosswalk, or on the subway, it's always kind to thank them for their service. But in the case of service members, we think being kind can go much further than a simple gesture. This year, find a service member—perhaps a veteran who lives in your neighborhood or the parent of someone you know at school—and ask if they'd be willing to tell you more about life in the military.

Here are a couple of sample questions you could ask to get the conversation started:

☆ Can you tell me where and when you served?

☆ How did your experience shape who you are today?

☆ What's a lasting memory from being deployed?

☆ What was the best part of being in the service?

☆ What was the most difficult part of being in the service?

Take what you learned and ask your teacher if you can share some of it with your classmates or share what you learned with your family over dinner. Every service member has something powerful to share and you can help pass it on. And be sure to write a thank you note to the service member after your interview concludes.

→ **What You May Need to Complete This Adventure:**

Access to a veteran or local service member
(Ask your school or neighbors if they have a friend or family member who would be willing to connect with you.)

Approximate time: one week or less

Cost: none

REPORT FROM THE FIELD

I completed this adventure on this date:

My adventure took place at:

I had help from the following people:

This adventure made me feel:

What I loved most about this adventure:

One thing I learned from this adventure:

One thing that surprised me about this adventure:

One thing I don't want to forget about this adventure:

Adventure 51

Write a Thank You Letter to Overseas Troops or First Responders

Have you ever been far from home and felt homesick, just wishing you could be in your bed or around your favorite things? For members of our military as well as first responders to natural disasters, they are often far from home for very long periods of time and homesickness is common.

That's why we love Operation Gratitude (operationgratitude.com) which has delivered more than 2.5 million care packages and gratitude boxes to active members of the military, veterans, first responders, and military families since its founding. Each care package is filled with items donated by grateful Americans and service-friendly companies who want to express their support for heroes serving overseas and here at home.

Work with your family or school community to host an Operation Gratitude collection and show your thanks in a special way to service members overseas and first responders here at home.

➡️ What You May Need to Complete This Adventure:

Support from friends and family to collect items for the gratitude drive

Access to the internet to explore most needed items from service members and first responders, which can be found on Operation Gratitude's website

Approximate time: one month or less

Cost: $–$$$

REPORT FROM THE FIELD

I completed this adventure on this date:

My adventure took place at:

I had help from the following people:

This adventure made me feel:

What I loved most about this adventure:

One thing I learned from this adventure:

One thing that surprised me about this adventure:

One thing I don't want to forget about this adventure:

Adventure 52

Help Our Troops Escape into a Good Book

For members of our military serving far from home, it can be hard to escape the daily stresses and challenges of life.

Operation Paperback (OperationPaperback.org) is another one of our favorite organizations—a national, non-profit organization whose volunteers collect gently used books and send them to American troops overseas, as well as to veterans, VA hospitals, and military families here at home. Since 1999, Operation Paperback has helped thousands of our troops escape into a good book and they've shipped more than 3 million books all over the world.

For this adventure, organize a book drive with your family, friends, or school through Operation Paperback and know that you'll be delivering kindness to troops and their families across the world.

→ **What You May Need to Complete This Adventure:**

Support from friends and family to collect items for the book drive

Access to the internet to explore details of organizing and planning a book drive for the troops

Approximate time: one month or less

Cost: none–$

REPORT FROM THE FIELD

I completed this adventure on this date:

My adventure took place at:

I had help from the following people:

This adventure made me feel:

What I loved most about this adventure:

One thing I learned from this adventure:

One thing that surprised me about this adventure:

One thing I don't want to forget about this adventure:

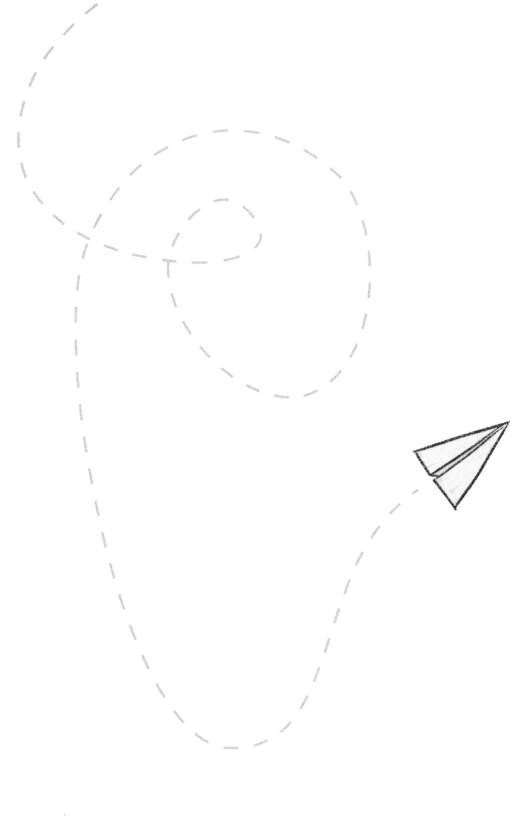

"I am only one,
But still I am one.
I cannot do everything,
But still I can do something;
And because I cannot
do everything,
I will not refuse to do the
something that I can do."

From *The Book of Good Cheer:
A Little Bundle of Cheery Thoughts* (1909)
by Edwin Osgood Grover

MORE GOOD THINGS

How to Say Hello in 35 Different Languages

1. Hi *(English)* / hai

2. Hallo *(Afrikaans)* / ha-lo

3. Tungjatjeta *(Albanian)* / toon-jah-TYEH-tah

4. مرحبا [Marhaban] *(Arabic)* / mar-ha-BAN

5. G'Day Mate *(Aussie)* / guh-day mate

6. Zdravo *(Bosnian)* / ZDRAH-voh

7. 你好 [Nǐ hǎo] *(Mandarin)* / nee how

8. Ahoj *(Czech)* / a-hoy

9. Hej *(Danish)* / hai

10. Hei *(Finnish)* / HAY

11. Bonjour *(French)* / bohn-ZHOOR

12. Γειά σου [Geiá sou] *(Greek)* / YAH soo

13. Alò *(Haitian Creole)* / a-LOW

a-Low

14. Aloha *(Hawaiian)* / a-lo-ha

15. नमस्ते [Namaste] *(Hindi)* / na-mas-tay

16. Halló *(Icelandic)* / hal-low

17. Dia duit *(Irish Gaelic)* / Jee-ah ghwitch

18. Ciao *(Italian)* / CHOW

19. こんにちは [Kon'nichiwa] *(Japanese)* / Kohn-nee-chee-wah

20. 안녕하세요 [Annyeonghaseyo] *(Korean)* / an-yong-has-ayo

21. Labas *(Lithuanian)* / LAH-bahs

22. Hei *(Norwegian)* / HAY

23. Ahoy *(Pirate)* / a-HOY

24. Olá *(Portugese)* / oh-LAH

25. Salut *(Romanian)* / sah-LOOT

26. Привет [Privet] *(Russian)* / pree-VYEHT

27. Zdravo *(Slovene/Slovanian)* / ZDRAH-voh

28. Hola *(Spanish)* / OH-lah

29. Jambo *(Swahili)* / jam-bo

30. Hej *(Swedish)* / HAY

31. Kamusta *(Tagalog)* / ka-moos-ta

32. Merhaba *(Turkish)* / mehr-HAH-bah

33. Helo *(Welsh)* / hel-lo

34. Sawubona *(Zulu)* / sawoo-bona

35. Hello *(American Sign Language)* / With your fingers extended, put your hand on your forehead and move it forward as if you were saluting.

Resource Guide 2
Great Books that Teach Empathy and Kindness

The following list of books was compiled by Ebony Elizabeth Thomas, Associate Professor at the University of Pennsylvania, who each week highlights authors and illustrators whose work deals with issues like gender, race, ethnicity, religion, sexuality, and socioeconomic class in ways that are real and empathetic.

Picture Books

⭐ *A Different Pond* (Bao Phi; illust. Thi Bui)

⭐ *Benny Doesn't Like To Be Hugged* (Zetta Elliott; illust. Purple Wong)

⭐ *Frida Kahlo and Her Animalitos* (Monica Brown; illust. John Parra)

⭐ *Hey Black Child* (Useni Eugene Perkins; illust. Bryan Collier)

⭐ *Little Leaders: Bold Women in Black History* (Vashti Harrison)

⭐ *Muddy: The Story of Blues Legend Muddy Waters* (Michael Mahin; illust. Evan Turk)

⭐ *Ruth Bader Ginsburg: The Case of R.B.G. vs. Inequality* (Jonah Winter; illust. Stacy Innerst)

⭐ *The People Shall Continue* (Simon J Ortiz; illust. Sharol Graves)

⭐ *Town Is by the Sea* (Joanne Schwartz; illust. Sydney Smith)

⭐ *The World Is Not a Rectangle: A Portrait of Architect Zaha Hadid* (Jeanette Winter)

⭐ *The Youngest Marcher: The Story of Audrey Faye Hendricks, a Young Civil Rights Activist* (Cynthia Levinson; illust. Vanessa Brantley-Newton)

⭐ *Yo Soy Muslim: A Father's Letter to His Daughter* (Mark Gonzales; illust. Mehrdokht Amini)

Middle Grade Fiction

- ✩ *Amina's Voice* (Hena Khan)

- ✩ *Clayton Byrd Goes Underground* (Rita Williams-Garcia)

- ✩ *Flying Lessons & Other Stories* (Edited by Ellen Oh)

- ✩ *It All Comes Down to This* (Karen English)

- ✩ *One Last Word: Wisdom from the Harlem Renaissance* (Nikki Grimes, illust. various artists)

- ✩ *Out of Wonder: Poems Celebrating Poets* (Kwame Alexander, Chris Colderley, Marjory Wentworth; illust. Ekua Holmes)

- ✩ *Piecing Me Together* (Renee Watson)

- ✩ *Rise of the Jumbies* (Tracey Baptiste)

- ✩ *See You in the Cosmos* (Jack Cheng)

- ✩ *Stef Soto, Taco Queen* (Jennifer Torres)

- ✩ *The First Rule of Punk* (Celia C. Pérez)

- ✩ *The Stars Beneath Our Feet* (David Barclay Moore)

Young Adult Fiction

- ✩ *American Street* (Ibi Zoboi)

- ✩ *City of Saints and Thieves* (Natalie Anderson)

- ✩ *Dear Martin* (Nic Stone)

- ✩ *Dreadnought* (April Daniels)

- ✩ *Saints and Misfits* (S.K. Ali)

- ✩ *Salt Houses* (Hala Alyan)

- ✩ *The Hate U Give* (Angie Thomas)

- ✩ *The Inexplicable Logic of My Life* (Benjamin Alire Sáenz)

☆ *The Marrow Thieves* (Cherie Dimaline)

☆ *They Both Die at the End* (Adam Silvera)

☆ *When Dimple Met Rishi* (Sandhya Menon)

☆ *You Bring the Distant Near* (Mitali Perkins)

Comics & Graphic Novels

☆ *America Vol. 1: The Life and Times of America Chavez* (Gabby Rivera, illust. Joe Quinones)

☆ *Black* (Kwanza Osajyefo; illust. Jamal Igle, Robin Riggs, Tim Smith III, Derwin Roberson, & Khary Randolph)

☆ *Brave* (Svetlana Chmakova)

☆ *I Am Alfonso Jones* (Tony Medina; illust. Stacey Robinson & John Jennings)

☆ *Kindred: A Graphic Novel Adaptation* (Octavia E. Butler; illust. John Jennings & Damian Duffy)

☆ *Love Is Love* (Marc Andreyko; edited by Sarah Gaydos & Jamie S. Rich)

☆ *Mighty Jack and the Goblin King*, Vol. 2 of the *Mighty Jack* series (Ben Hatke; illust. Ben Hatke, Alex Campbell & Hilary Sycamore)

☆ *The Best We Could Do: An Illustrated Memoir* (Thi Bui)

☆ *Where's Halmoni?* (Julie Kim)

☆ *Wires and Nerve*, Volume 1 (Marissa Meyer, Stephen Gilpin)

Special thanks to Penn GSE students Rabani Garg, James Joshua Coleman, Jacqueline R. Dawson, and Doricka Menefee who assisted Thomas in reviewing children's books throughout 2017 and in compiling this list.

Index of Organizations Mentioned in this Book

Active
Global
Active.com
ActiveKids.com

Bikes for the World
Rockville, MD
bikesfortheworld.org/get-involved/
how-to-organize-a-collection

Cards for Hospitalized Kids
Chicago, IL
cardsforhospitalizedkids.com

Comfort Cases
Rockville, MD
comfortcases.org

Deanna F. Cook
Northampton, Massachusetts
Cooking Class, a kid's cookbook
deannafcook.com/cooking-class

Hope for Henry
Washington, DC
hopeforhenry.org

Hungry Harvest
Baltimore, MD
HungryHarvest.net

Imperfect Foods
San Francisco, CA
ImperfectFoods.com

Little Free Library
Hudson, WI
littlefreelibrary.org

Lollipop Kids Foundation
Rockville, MD
lollipopkidsfoundation.org

Meatless Monday
Baltimore, MD
MeatlessMonday.com

Misfits Market
Philadelphia, PA
MisfitsMarket.com

National Park Service
Washington, DC
nps.gov

National Wildlife Federation
Reston, VA
nwf.org/NativePlantFinder

Operation Gratitude
Encino, CA
operationgratitude.com

Operation Paperback
York, PA
OperationPaperback.org

Ronald McDonald Houses
Chicago, IL
rmhc.org

Donald Silver and
Patricia Wynne
New York, NY
One Small Square book series

St. Jude Children's
Research Hospital
Memphis, TN
stjude.org

Teaching Tolerance
Montgomery, AL
www.tolerance.org/mix-it-up

Together We Rise
Brea, CA
togetherwerise.org

Veggie Kids
San Francisco, CA
Veggie-kids.com

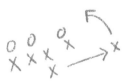

Index of Adventures

Adventures for Your Health

Adventures for Our World

Adventures for Your Mind

Endnotes

1   Adventure One: PETA Kids. "How You Can Help Animals in Shelters." https://www.petakids.com/save-animals/help-shelter-animals/.

2   Adventure Two: Parker, Laura. "Straw Wars: The Fight to Rid the Oceans of Discarded Plastic." *National Geographic*, February 23, 2018. https://www.nationalgeographic.com/news/2017/04/plastic-straws-ocean-trash-environment/.

3   Adventure Two: World Economic Forum. *The New Plastics Economy: Rethinking the future of plastics*. REF 080116, January 2016. http://www3.weforum.org/docs/WEF_The_New_Plastics_Economy.pdf.

4   Adventure Eight: United States Department of Health and Human Services. "Adoption & Foster Care Statistics." Children's Bureau, 2018. https://www.acf.hhs.gov/cb/research-data-technology/statistics-research/afcars.

5   Adventure Twenty Two: United States Environmental Protection Agency. "Showerheads." https://www.epa.gov/watersense/showerheads.

6   Adventure Twenty Eight: Mekonnen, Mesfin and Arjen Hoekstra. "The green, blue and grey water footprint of farm animals and animal products." Delft, the Netherlands : Unesco-IHE Institute for Water Education, 2010.

7   Adventure Twenty Eight: Leahy, Stephen. "Choosing chicken over beef cuts our carbon footprints a surprising amount." *National Geographic*, June 10, 2019. https://www.nationalgeographic.com/environment/2019/06/choosing-chicken-over-beef-cuts-carbon-footprint-surprising-amount/.

8   Adventure Thirty Three: Panetta, Grace and Olivia Reane. "Today is National Voter Registration Day. The evolution of American voting rights in 242 years shows how far we've come—and how far we still have to go." *Business Insider*, September 24, 2019. https://www.businessinsider.com/when-women-got-the-right-to-vote-american-voting-rights-timeline-2018-10.

9   Adventure Thirty Three: UC Santa Barbara. "Voter Turnout in Presidential Elections." The American Presidency Project. https://www.presidency.ucsb.edu/statistics/data/voter-turnout-in-presidential-elections.

10   Adventure Forty Five: World Economic Forum. *The New Plastics Economy: Rethinking the future of plastics*. REF 080116, January 2016. http://www3.weforum.org/docs/WEF_The_New_Plastics_Economy.pdf.

Congratulations!

YOU'VE MADE KIND LOOK AWESOME

If you've completed at least five adventures in this book, you've officially made it to the ranks of the Adventures in Kindness Kids Club. And if you've completed at least 25 adventures in this book, you have mastered the Kindness Challenge. Your job now is to pass it on. Take all that you learned, and share it with others. Bring these kindness adventures out into the world with you, and let them set off even more kind deeds.

If you've loved the adventures in this book, and you're ready for more, ask your family if you can head on over to our website to join the official Adventures in Kindness Kids Club, access your free sticker or backpack badge, and check out more cool adventures and resources for you, your family, your community and your school.

adventuresinkindness.com

Have you taken on a kindness adventure not included in this book? Be sure to submit it to us via the website and you could be featured in our next book!

WE'RE PROUD OF YOU, KID, AND WE KNOW THIS IS JUST THE BEGINNING OF MORE GOOD THINGS TO COME.

Acknowledgments

From the Authors:

To Nichole—our partner from day one on this project. You jumped into this book without even fully knowing what it would become, and captured exactly the spirit of kindness, creativity, and inclusion we imagined. There's no illustrator in the world more incredible than you—and how lucky we are that you were ours!

To our test readers—Lilia and her mom Kathy, Sean and his mom Annica, Ms. Tsakos, Ms. Heald, Tara D'uva, and Nana Carol. Your edits, insights, and encouragement were so important. Your kind hearts inspired so many of the special details inside this book.

To Girl Scout Troop 33005—the 13 amazing girls who served as founding members of our Adventures in Kindness Kids Club, who helped test many of the adventures featured in the book, and who inspired many of the items in our kindness store. Your sweet hearts and smart, curious questions made such a difference in the development of this book.

To our amazing friends and colleagues at Mission Partners—especially Eleni Stamoulis, Anne Kerns, Isabel Linder, Bayonia Marshall, and Kristine Neil—for helping us bring an idea to life in ways far beyond we could have ever imagined. Your passion and enthusiasm for this project was contagious.

To Baxter and Malcolm—for inspiring the animal adventures in this book and for serving as such wonderful muses to the pup illustrations inside these pages.

To Flower Child—the best little café, in which most of this book was written, for giving us the most delicious and nourishing spot to put our adventures on paper.

To all the nonprofits in this book as well as those we've had the opportunity to partner with and learn from over the years. It's your big acts of kindness that have inspired so many little acts of our own.

And, with the biggest thanks of all—to Brian and Kate for giving us so much love and time to work on this project together. There was nothing more fun than going on the adventures in this book with you two. Thanks for inspiring kindness through your actions, and for being the most wonderful Papa and sister. We love you so much.

From the Illustrator:

To PJ, thank you for supporting me through all the late nights and early mornings, you are my rock. To Mia and Mason, my muses. Thank you to all my family, especially my sister, Ali, who provides a guiding light. Special thanks to Carrie and Sophia without your wonderful ideas there would be no book to fill with illustrations.

"Help people.
Be a good person.
In the end,
nothing else
matters."

Pop Pop Bob Fox
1943 – 2011

NOTES

CPSIA information can be obtained
at www.ICGtesting.com
Printed in the USA
LVHW010801140820
663081LV00014B/2240